SCIENCE ACADEMY

# SCIENTIST

## IN TRAINING

SCIENCE ACADEMY

# STUDENT PASS

# KINGFISHER
LONDON & NEW YORK

Copyright © Macmillan Publishers International Ltd 2018
Published in the United States by Kingfisher.
175 Fifth Ave., New York, NY 10010
Kingfisher is an imprint of Macmillan Children's Books, London

Distributed in the U.S. and Canada by Macmillan.
175 Fifth Ave., New York, NY 10010

Library of Congress Cataloging-in-Publication data has been applied for.

Series editor: Hayley Down
Designer: Jeni Child
Author: Cath Ard
Illustrator: Sarah Lawrence

ISBN 978-0-7534-7443-3

Kingfisher books are available for special promotions and premiums.
For details contact: Special Markets Department, Macmillan,
175 Fifth Ave., New York, NY 10010.

For more information, please visit
www.kingfisherbooks.com

Printed in China
9 8 7 6 5 4 3 2 1
1TR/0618/WKT/UG/128MA

Picture credits
The Publisher would like to thank the following for permission to reproduce their material.
Top = t; Bottom = b; Center = c; Left = l; Right = r
Pages 18tl Shutterstock/Anna Om; 18br Shutterstock/Mike Mareen; 19tl iStock/kemter; 19cr Shutterstock/Vasin Lee;
24tr Shutterstock/Jos Beltman; 24cl Shutterstock/Volodymyr Burdiak; 24br Shutterstock/Fotos593;
25tl Shutterstock/Alexey Seafarer; 25cr Shutterstock/Chakorn Amornset; 25br Shutterstock/EpicStockMedia;
26tl Shutterstock/Cathy Keifer; 26cl iStock/KeithSzaFranski; 27tl Shutterstock/StevenRussellSmithPhotos;
27cl iStock/Somogyvari; 40 (cotton) Shutterstock/RobD Photography; 40 (gold) Shutterstock/MarcelClemens;
40 (clay) Shutterstock/Lone Pine; 40 (wool) Shutterstock/foto76; 40 (wood) Shutterstock/Suti Stock Photo;
40 (chalk) Shutterstock/Tyler Boyes; 40 (leather) Shutterstock/Hazem.m.kamai; 40 (stone) Shutterstock/Kinkku;
41 (paper) Shutterstock/ESB Professional; 41 (concrete) Shutterstock/Black Digital Cat; 41 (nylon) Shutterstock/
iceink; 41 (plastic) Shutterstock/EVGENIYA68; 41 (glass) Shutterstock/Mark Agnor; 41 (steel) Shutterstock/boonchai
sakunchonruedee; 41 (cardboard) Shutterstock/LyubovF; 41 (brick) Shutterstock/Tomasz Mazon; 43tl Alamy/Science
History Images; 43br Alamy/WENN Ltd.

# SCIENTIST

## IN TRAINING

KINGFISHER
LONDON & NEW YORK

# SCIENCE ACADEMY

# TRAINING PROGRAM

# TRAINING TIME

So you want to be a scientist? Do you like asking questions and looking closely at things? Do you love doing experiments and making discoveries? Then science is perfect for you.

## HOW TO BE A SCIENTIST

You will need to study hard and follow these rules . . .

**1** Look very closely at things

**2** Ask questions

**3** Have ideas

**4** Do experiments

**5** Record your results

## ACTIVITY

Find five differences between the two pictures.

Can you find the mouse on each page?

# WHAT IS SCIENCE?

Science is the study of the world around us. There's a lot to learn, so put on your white lab coat and start by finding out what science is all about.

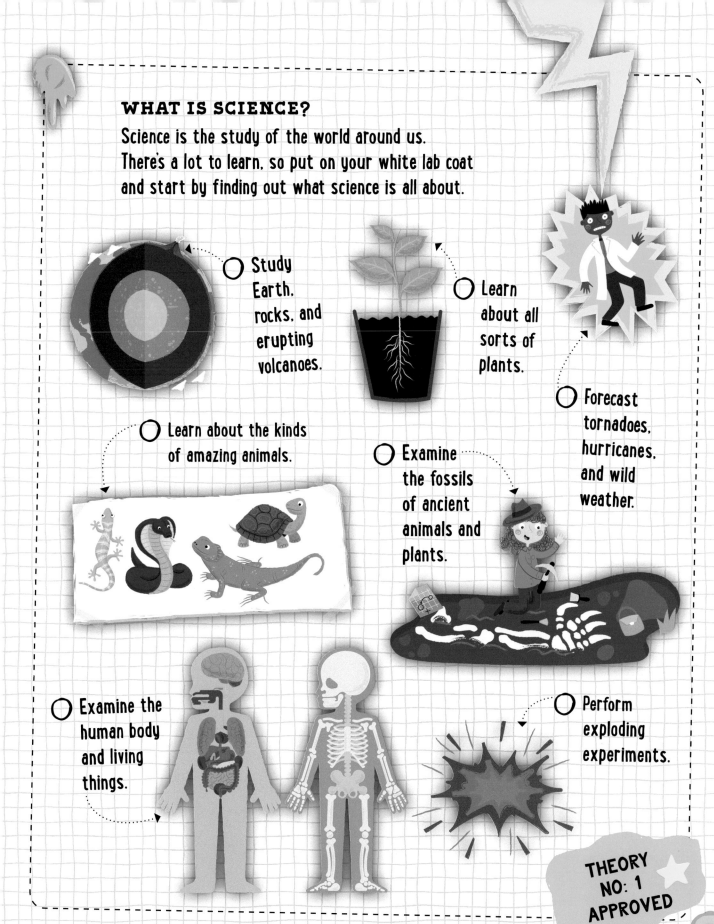

○ Study Earth, rocks, and erupting volcanoes.

○ Learn about all sorts of plants.

○ Forecast tornadoes, hurricanes, and wild weather.

○ Learn about the kinds of amazing animals.

○ Examine the fossils of ancient animals and plants.

○ Examine the human body and living things.

○ Perform exploding experiments.

THEORY NO: 1 APPROVED

# SCIENCE KIT

Scientists use lots of equipment to help them with their experiments. Before you start your training, you need to collect some useful stuff from the science lab.

## EQUIPMENT

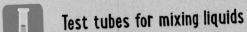 Safety glasses to protect eyes from splashes

Test tubes for mixing liquids

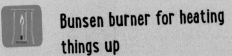 Bunsen burner for heating things up

Computer for recording results

Microscope for seeing small things close up

Scales for weighing objects

This scientist needs to weigh a dinosaur bone. Find the thing he needs to help him.

## ACTIVITY

Can you find these things in the busy labaratory?

➡ magnifying glass ➡ pencil
➡ ruler ➡ notebook

PRACTICAL NO: 1 APPROVED

# EARTH

 Earth is our planet. It is covered with huge salty oceans, big rocky lands, and sandy islands.

Earth is a giant ball made up of different layers. If you sliced into it, it would look like this.

## CRUST
The outer rocky layer that we live on is called the crust.

## MANTLE
The mantle is a layer of sticky, moving rock below the crust.

## HOW FAR HAVE WE EXPLORED?
Deep holes have been dug, but none have reached the bottom of Earth's crust. The biggest hole is about 7 mi (12 km) deep—14 of the world's tallest skyscrapers piled one on top of the other could fit inside it. It gets hotter and hotter the deeper you go.

## VOLCANOES

A volcano is an opening in Earth's crust. When a volcano **erupts**, hot, runny rock called **magma** escapes from deep inside Earth.

## ACTIVITY

Earth is made of many types of rock. Different rocks are used for different things. Join each rock with the thing it is used for.

Clay is soft when wet and hard when dry.

Slate breaks into thin pieces.

Chalk is soft and crumbly.

## OUTER CORE
The outer core is boiling hot, melted metal.

## INNER CORE
The inner core is solid metal.

THEORY NO: 2 APPROVED

# FOSSILS

Clues about how Earth looked millions of years ago are hidden under your feet. Scientists have discovered **fossils** of animals that lived long ago ... It's time for a dino dig!

## WHAT DO FOSSILS TELL US?

Scientists can figure out what dinosaurs looked like by putting fossil pieces back together, just like a puzzle.

This Tyrannosaurus rex was a fierce meat-eater.

## HOW IS A FOSSIL MADE?

**1** When a dinosaur died, its body became covered with mud.

**2** The soft body rotted away, but the hard bones were left behind.

**3** Over time, the mud and bones became hard and turned to stone.

Fossils tell us how the world has changed. Fish fossils found in deserts show that very dry places were once covered by a lake or river.

fishy fossil ·········

Pick the correct fossil bones to complete this dinosaur skeleton.

1
2
3
4
5
6
7
8
9

a
b
c
d
e

PRACTICAL NO: 2 APPROVED

# SEASONS

The weather can be:

sunny

hot

rainy

windy

frosty

snowy

**Which words describe the weather in each season where you live?**

The weather can be:

sunny

hot

rainy

windy

frosty

snowy

## SPRING

Blossoms and new leaves grow on some trees.

Can you spot these things?

 leaf buds

 blossoms

 bird building nest

## SUMMER

The trees are covered in green leaves.

Can you spot these things?

 flowers

 bees

ladybug

The weather changes with the seasons. In most countries, there are four seasons: spring, summer, fall, and winter.

PRACTICAL NO: 3 APPROVED

The weather can be:

sunny

hot

rainy

windy

frosty

snowy

Plants change with the seasons, too!

The weather can be:

sunny

hot

rainy

windy

frosty

snowy

## FALL

The leaves of most trees turn brown and fall to the ground.

Can you spot these things?

- chestnut
- squirrel
- mushrooms

## WINTER

Many trees have bare branches. But some trees stay green all year.

Can you spot these things?

- bird
- berries
- evergreen tree

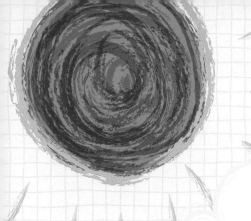

Water droplets in the air form clouds.

**1 SUN**

The Sun heats up the water in lakes, rivers, and on the ground. As it heats up, water turns into tiny droplets that are too small to see.

**2 CLOUDS**

The droplets float up into the air. They group together in the sky to make clouds.

**3 RAIN**

When enough droplets have gathered together, the cloud becomes heavy and it rains.

Raindrops flow into rivers or oceans.

PRACTICAL 4

# WATER CYCLE

Water is amazing! Next time you are taking a bath, just think: this is the same water that dinosaurs swam in! That's because every drop of water on Earth has been here for billions of years.

As the clouds rise, they get colder and rain falls.

**5 START AGAIN**
Then the Sun warms up the water . . . and the cycle starts again.

**4 GROUND**
The rain soaks into the ground, runs down the rivers, and flows into the lakes and oceans.

Streams and rivers flow downhill.

Rivers flow back into the ocean.

**EXPERIMENT**

Put some water in a cup and mark to show where it reaches. Leave the cup out in the sunshine. Check it after a day—some water will have turned into tiny droplets and floated into the air!

# WEATHER

Time to step out of the science lab and study the weather. Is it hot, windy, rainy, or snowy outside?

The Sun is really a star!

## SUN

On clear days, the warmth from the Sun heats up the land.

## RAINBOWS

Colorful rainbows are made by the sunlight shining through water droplets in the air.

## WIND

Wind is moving air. You can't see it, but you can feel it blowing.

## FOG

On a foggy day you are walking through cloud that has come right down to the ground.

A fogbow is a bit like a rainbow, except you see it when sunlight shines through fog.

## SHAPE OF SNOWFLAKES

All snowflakes have six sides, but every snowflake is different. The temperature of the sky as snowflakes fall causes them to grow different patterns.

snowy mountains

## SNOW AND HAIL

When water droplets in clouds freeze, they fall as snow or hail.

## LIGHTNING AND THUNDER

Lightning is electricity that is made in a storm cloud. It flashes down to the ground. A rumble of thunder comes after lightning.

lightning

## HURRICANES

Scientists study pictures of Earth taken from space to see what weather is coming our way. This picture shows a big swirling storm, called a hurricane.

Every hurricane is given a boy's or girl's name. Name this hurricane!

19

# PLANTS

Plants are living things.
They can be tiny weeds or giant
trees. Plants stay in one place,
but they grow and change,
just like you do.

**GROWING SEEDS**

When a seed is safely in the ground, it splits open and a root and a shoot push out.

The root reaches down to find water and the shoot reaches up to find light.

A stem and leaves grow from the shoot.

**MAKING SEEDS**

Lots of plants grow flowers. They make a juice called **nectar** and a sticky powder called pollen to attract bees.

When a bee visits a flower, pollen sticks to the bee.

When the bee flies to the next flower, some pollen rubs off and the flower can grow seeds.

## SPREADING SEEDS

## EXPERIMENT

Ask an adult to cut an apple in half for you. Can you see the seeds inside?

Most plants grow from a seed. Seeds need to spread for new plants to grow.

Some seeds float on the breeze.

Some grow in pods that burst.

Some are inside the fruit that is eaten (and pooped out!) by animals.

Some have tiny hooks that get stuck to passing animals and drop off in another place.

# ANIMALS

Our planet is home to millions of different kinds of animals. They come in all shapes and sizes.

## MAMMALS

All mammals breathe air. Whales and dolphins breathe through a special nostril called a blowhole. Most mammals give birth to live babies and feed them with their milk.

## REPTILES

Reptiles have dry, scaly skin. Some give birth to live babies, but most lay eggs. They lie in the sun to warm up and hide in the shade to cool down.

## FISH

Fish live in oceans, ponds, streams, and rivers. Fish breathe water. They take **oxygen** out of the water with special slits in their sides called **gills**.

## INVERTEBRATES

These insects, creepy-crawlies, and mollusks are animals that don't have a backbone. Some have a hard outer shell, and others have a soft, slimy body.

## BIRDS

All birds lay eggs. They have a beak, feathers, two legs, and two wings. Most birds can fly, some can swim, and some just walk or run.

## AMPHIBIANS

(say am-fib-ee-ans)
Amphibians can live on land or in the water. Most of them lay eggs in or near water. Many have thin, moist skin. They cool off in the water and warm up in the sun.

## ACTIVITY

Match each animal with its correct animal group.

**THEORY 4**

# HABITATS

Record the wild animals that live in habitats near you.

Every plant and animal on Earth lives in the place that suits it best. This is called a **habitat**. There are lots of different habitats to explore.

## DESERT

Deserts are very dry places. The plants and animals that live here can survive with very little food or water.

## GRASSLAND

There is not enough rain for many trees to grow here, but there is lots of grass for herds of animals to eat. Big meat eaters hunt here, too!

## RAIN FOREST

It is rainy and hot here—perfect for plants to grow. Millions of big and small creatures live here, feasting on the fruit—and on each other!

## POLAR LAND

It is very cold here and covered in snow and ice. Animals that live here have thick fur or layers of fat to keep them warm.

## WETLAND

These rain-soaked places are filled with water-loving trees, plants, and animals.

## CORAL REEF

Corals are animals, but they look like colorful underwater plants. They live in warm, shallow waters. They provide food and homes for lots of ocean life.

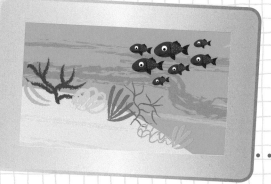

## OCEAN

Oceans cover most of our planet. They are filled with sunlight at the top, but are dark and cold in the deepest places.

THEORY
NO: 4
APPROVED

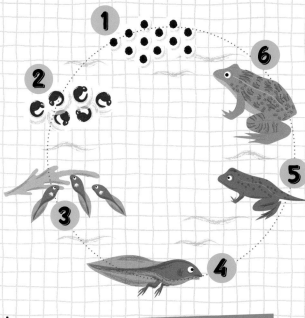

## FROG

**1** A female frog lays her eggs in water.

**2** A tadpole grows inside each egg.

**3** The tadpoles hatch and then swim and eat.

**4** Each tadpole grows legs.

**5** The tadpole becomes a froglet.

**6** The froglet loses its tail and becomes a frog.

## THEORY 5

# LIFE CYCLES

Animals have babies, which grow and change as they get older. When they are fully grown, they have babies of their own. This is called a life cycle.

## PENGUIN

**1** A female penguin lays an egg.

**2** The male penguin sits on the egg to keep it warm.

**3** A tiny chick grows inside the egg.

**4** The chick is ready to hatch.

**5** The chick pecks the shell open with its beak.

**6** The chick walks, eats, and grows.

## BUTTERFLY

**1** A female butterfly lays eggs on a leaf.

**2** A caterpillar grows inside each egg.

**3** The caterpillars hatch and then eat lots and lots of leaves.

**4** The caterpillar makes a **cocoon** of soft threads around itself.

**5** Inside the cocoon the caterpillar grows legs and wings.

**6** A butterfly climbs out of the cocoon and flies away.

## 🍃 ACTVITY

Human babies grow inside their mother. Which of these life cycles is the same?

## THEORY NO: 5 APPROVED

**MAMMAL**

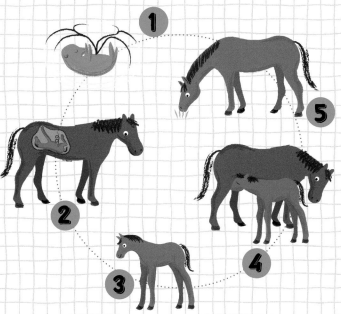

## HORSE

**1** An egg inside the mommy horse begins to grow.

**2** A tiny foal grows inside the mommy.

**3** The foal is born. It can stand and walk.

**4** The foal drinks its mother's milk.

**5** The foal grows bigger and eats grass.

## PRACTICAL 7

# YOUR BODY

Your body has thousands of different parts, and each one has an important job to do. Many parts are working inside you right now without you having to think about them.

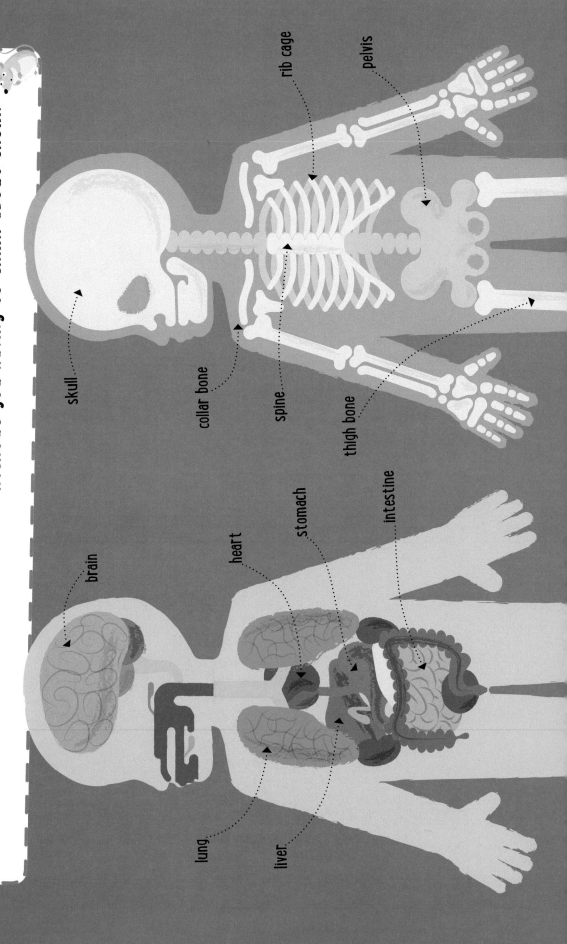

rib cage

pelvis

skull

collar bone

spine

thigh bone

brain

heart

stomach

intestine

lung

liver

kneecap

Your bones make a strong frame for your body, called a skeleton. It protects your organs and helps you move.

## ACTIVITY

Can you find these bones on the skeleton? Find them on your own body, too!

tibia

humerus

rib

## EXPERIMENT

When you move, your heart has to work harder to carry energy to your muscles.

Jump up and down for 30 seconds. Put your hand on your chest—can you feel your heart thumping? Stay still and feel the beat slow down.

PRACTICAL NO: 7 APPROVED

Organs inside you perform different jobs. Your lungs breathe air and your heart pumps your blood.

## CAN YOU FIND?

Brain: this controls your whole body.

Heart: this pumps blood around your body.

Lungs: these take air into your body.

Liver: this cleans your blood.

Stomach: this holds the food that you eat.

Intestines: food is broken down here for your body to use.

# YOUR SENSES

As soon as you wake up in the morning, your five senses start telling you what's going on around you.

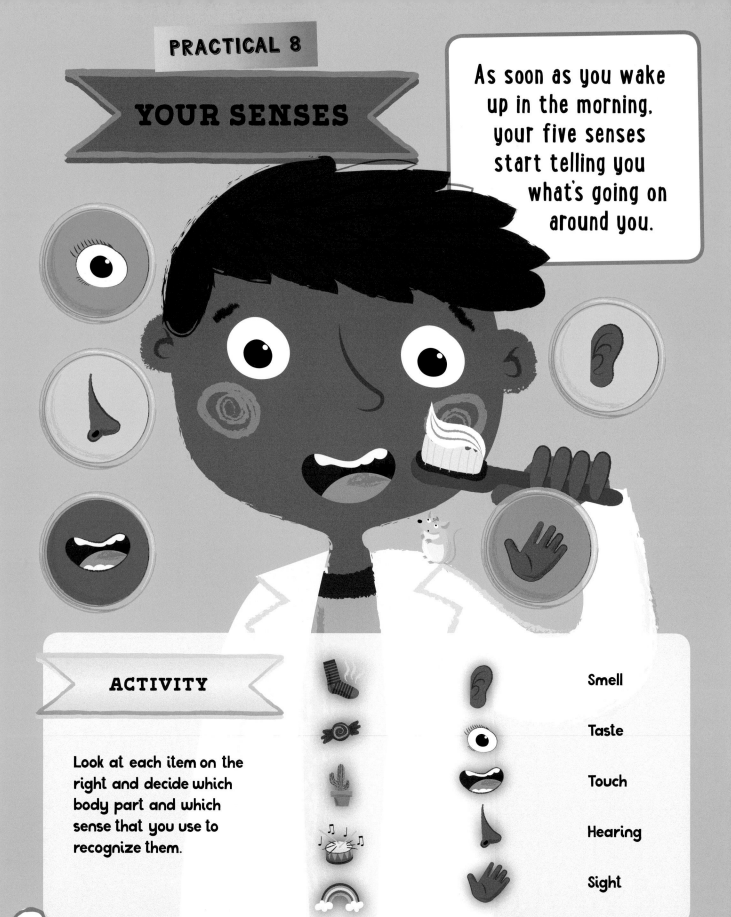

## ACTIVITY

Look at each item on the right and decide which body part and which sense that you use to recognize them.

Smell

Taste

Touch

Hearing

Sight

30

## SEEING

You need light to see things. Light goes into your eyes through your **pupils**.

## HEARING

Sounds are ripples, or vibrations, in the air that travel into your ears. Your brain turns them into sounds.

## SMELL

When something is smelly, tiny parts of it float into the air. Your nose recognizes the smells when you breathe in the tiny parts.

## TOUCH

You feel with the skin all over your body. It tells you whether things are hot or cold, soft, hard, or sharp.

## TASTE

Tiny taste buds on your tongue tell you if food or drink is sweet, salty, bitter, or sour.

## UNDER THE MICROSCOPE

Look in the mirror and stick out your tongue. It's okay, it's for science! Can you see the dots? Those are your taste buds. Here they are close up.

# SOUND

From ticking clocks to tweeting birds, your world is filled with sound. Close your eyes and listen. Now open your eyes again—it's time for some science!

A chiming clock has a low pitch. BONG!

## SCIENCE EXPERIMENT

Sounds are made when objects vibrate, or move quickly back and forth. The vibrations make the air around them vibrate too. We can't see sounds, but you can see the vibrations with this experiment.

**1** Stretch some plastic wrap over a bowl.

**2** Put some grains of sugar on the top.

**3** Put your face close to the bowl and hum.

**4** The vibrations in the air make the grains of sugar jump.

"Hmmmmmmm!"

A tweeting bird has a high pitch. Tweet! Tweet!

# LIGHT

Switch on your science brain and investigate light. Light lets you see the world around you. Check out the different things that make light.

## DAYLIGHT
During the day, most of the light comes from the Sun.

## ARTIFICIAL LIGHT
When it's dark, we switch on electric lights so we can see inside and outside.

Things that burn give off light, too.

Some animals make light, such as this glowworm.

Cars have lights so drivers can see and be seen.

Gadgets with screens give off light.

GIANT SNAIL FOUND

_____

_____

## REFLECTIONS

At night, the Moon reflects the Sun's light.

Water, mirrors, and metal reflect light too.

## ACTIVITY

When light hits a solid object, it blocks the light. This creates a shadow. Shadows are usually a similar shape to the object that casts them.

Pick the correct shadow for this snail.

A

B

C

## SEE-THROUGH

If light can shine through an object it is see-through, or **transparent**.

Try making a snail shadow with your hands.

Can you help the scientist reach his cycling friend?

## THEORY 8

# FORCES

Objects need a force to get them moving.
A force can be a push, a pull, or a twist.

THEORY
NO: 8
APPROVED

## ACTIVITY

These scientists are having fun at the park, but they are also studying forces.

Decide what kind of force is being used in each activity.

PUSH          PULL          TWIST

# INVISIBLE FORCES

Ready for some science magic? Some forces are invisible. They can move objects without touching them!

## MAGNETS

A magnet is a piece of metal that can pull some types of metal toward it. Metals that stick to a magnet are **magnetic**.

2 + 2 =

Use a fridge magnet to test these objects to see if they are magnetic.

## IS IT MAGNETIC?

|  |  | Y or N? |
|---|---|---|
| 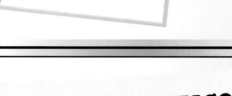 | book | N |
|  | fork | Y |
|  | paperclip | Y |
|  | eraser | N |
|  | saucepan | Y |
|  | aluminum foil | Y |
|  | glass | N |
|  | coin | N |

## GRAVITY

**Gravity** is the invisible force that keeps your feet on the ground. When you jump up in the air, you fall back down again. That's because Earth is pulling you toward its surface.

astronaut

Gravity brings you back to Earth!

I am too far away to be pulled by Earth's gravity, so I float.

## EXPERIMENT

**1** Take a piece of thread and tie one end to a paperclip and the other end to a pencil.

**2** Hold the pencil straight, and the paperclip points down because gravity is pulling it. What happens if you tilt the pencil?

# PRACTICAL 10

# MATERIALS

The objects we use every day are made from materials. A material can be hard, soft, strong, stiff, flexible, light, or heavy.

## NATURAL MATERIALS

cotton
wood
gold
chalk
clay
leather
wool
stone

Natural materials are found on our planet. They come from plants, animals, and rocks. Help the scientist find the natural materials on the shelves above.

## ACTIVITY

🍃 Hunt for different materials in the science lab. Can you see the things listed on the chart?

| ROCK | GLASS | PLASTIC | METAL | PAPER |
|------|-------|---------|-------|-------|
| Statue | Drinking glass | Pail | Necklace | Book |
| Chalkboard | Building | Shovel | Kettle | Pizza box |

## ARTIFICIAL MATERIALS

paper

glass

concrete

steel

nylon

cardboard

plastic

brick

Artificial materials are made by humans. Some are made from natural materials. Paper is made from wood. Glass is made from sand. Help the scientist find the artificial materials on the shelf above.

### LEONARDO DA VINCI

Leonardo was an Italian inventor and artist. He drew plans for a helicopter hundreds of years before they were invented.

### MARY ANNING

Mary was a famous fossil hunter. She discovered fossils of dinosaurs and ancient animals in the cliffs near her seaside home in Dorset, England.

### SIR ISAAC NEWTON

Newton discovered gravity when he saw an apple fall from a tree. This made him realize there was a force that pulled things to the ground.

### GEORGE WASHINGTON CARVER

Carver was a botanist, which meant he studied plants. He pioneered new ways of farming so that poor farmers could grow their own food.

# HALL OF FAME

## LOUIS PASTEUR

Pasteur discovered that germs cause disease. This helped him create vaccinations to keep people from getting sick.

## MARIE CURIE

Marie Curie helped to invent X-ray machines, which take pictures of the bones inside your body.

## ALBERT EINSTEIN

Einstein is one of the world's most famous scientists. He realized that nothing in the universe travels faster than light.

## TIM BERNERS-LEE

Computer scientist Tim Berners-Lee created the World Wide Web—the pages of information that you can see on your computer.

These brilliant scientists all made discoveries and inventions that changed the world.

# EXAMINATION

## Now it's time to see how much you have learned.

**1** What is the name of the rocky layer on the outside of Earth?
a) The crust
b) The coast
c) The crumb

**2** What is the name of the runny rock inside a volcano?
a) Mega
b) Magma
c) Molten

**3** What are fossils?
a) Bones that have turned to dust
b) Bones that have turned to mud
c) Bones that have turned to stone

**4** In which season would you find leaf buds and blossoms?
a) Fall
b) Summer
c) Spring

**5** What are clouds made from?
a) Water droplets
b) Air bubbles
c) Smoke

**6** Which of these sentences is TRUE?
a) Snowflakes are all different.
b) Snowflakes are all the same.

**7** What are hurricanes?
a) Big rivers
b) Big storms
c) Big waves

**8** Which of these is FALSE?
a) Fish don't breathe.
b) Fish breathe water.

**9** Where can you find coral?
a) In a desert
b) In a forest
c) In the ocean

**10** What is the sticky powder in flowers called?
  a) Pollen
  b) Honey
  c) Sugar

**11** Which part of your body pumps the blood around?
  a) The lungs
  b) The heart
  c) The brain

**12** Where is your spine?
  a) In your head
  b) In your back
  c) In your hip

**13** What is the name of the things on your tongue that help you taste?
  a) Tasty bods
  b) Taste buddies
  c) Taste buds

**14** Which of these things is transparent?
  a) A drinking glass
  b) Some metal
  c) Some wood

**15** Which of these objects is magnetic?
  a) Paper
  b) Paperclip
  c) Sticky tape

## SCIENCE SCORES

Check your answers at the back of the book and add up your score.

**1 to 5** Oops! Get back to the lab and study up on your science facts.

**6 to 10** You are well on your way to becoming a super scientist.

**11 to 15** Top of the class! You could be the next Einstein!

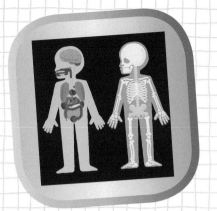

# SCIENCE SPEAK

### cocoon
The covering of soft threads that protects some insects as they change into an adult.

### erupt
When a volcano erupts, it explodes and hot, runny rock bursts out of it.

### fossil
The shape of an old bone, shell, or plant that has turned to rock.

### gills
The slits through which fish and other water creatures breathe.

### gravity
The invisible force that makes things fall to the ground on Earth.

### habitat
The natural surroundings where different plants or animals live.

### magma
Hot rock that is found deep under the surface of Earth.

### magnetic
Describes a material that is pulled toward a magnet.

**nectar**
A sweet juice made by flowers to attract bees and other insects. Bees make nectar into honey.

**organs**
Important parts inside your body that have a special job to do.

**oxygen**
The gas in the air that plants and animals need to live.

**pupil**
The dark circle in the middle of the eye that lets in light.

**transparent**
Describes something you can see through clearly.

**vaccination**
A special treatment that stops a person or animal from catching a disease.

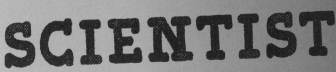

SCIENCE ACADEMY

# WELL DONE!

You made it through your scientist training.

FULLY QUALIFIED

# SCIENTIST

# ANSWERS

## Page 6
The five differences are:

## Page 8
The things to find are circled below.

## Page 13
a = 7
b = 2
c = 8
d = 5
e = 4

## Page 23
The frog is an amphibian.
The bear is a mammal.
The blue fish is a fish.
The millipede is an invertebrate.
The puffin is a bird.

## Page 27
Humans are mammals: their life cycle is similar to a horse's.

## Page 29
The things to find are circled below.

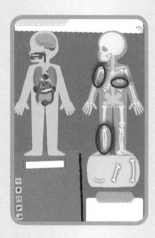

## Page 33
The things to find are circled below.

## Page 35
The correct shadow is A.

## Page 36
Kicking a ball = push
Sliding on a slide = pull
Twirling on a merry-go-round = twist
A dog pulling its lead = pull
Pushing a boy on a swing = push

## Page 41
cotton = T-shirt
wood = chair
gold = necklace
chalk = chalkboard
clay = vase
leather = shoe
wool = ball of yarn
stone = statue
paper = book
glass = drinking glass
concrete = building
steel = kettle
nylon = swimsuit
cardboard = pizza box
plastic = pail and shovel
brick = house

## Page 44
1 = a; 2 = b; 3 = c; 4 = c; 5 = a;
6 = a; 7 = b; 8 = a; 9 = c; 10 = a;
11 = b; 12 = b; 13 = c; 14 = a; 15 = b.